T0194631

MESSAGES FROM FLOWERS

IGAEGBURUMNWA EMMANUEL

illustrated by

Iwueke Kelechi

authorHOUSE®

AuthorHouse™
1663 Liberty Drive
Bloomington, IN 47403
www.authorhouse.com
Phone: 1 (800) 839-8640

Published by AuthorHouse 09/27/2019

ISBN: 978-1-7283-2240-7 (sc)
ISBN: 978-1-7283-2239-1 (e)

Library of Congress Control Number: 2019912219

Print information available on the last page.

Any people depicted in stock imagery provided by Getty Images are models, and such images are being used for illustrative purposes only. Certain stock imagery © Getty Images.

This book is printed on acid-free paper.

Poetry is the renewal of words, setting them free, and that's what a poet is doing: loosening the words.-Robert Frost.

We are more of souls than body. Poetry is important to the soul as air is important to the body.

Money, houses, cars and clothes are things necessary to sustain life. But poetry, beauty, love, romance and music are the things necessary to keep us alive because they nourish the soul. Everything comes from the soul; Healing, love and intimacy all comes from the soul.

Poetry are words that comforts the soul with its mild voice streamlining through the vein as it passes directly from the ear to the brain supplying serenity to the mind and body.

-Igacgburumnwa Emmanuel

Thanks to Iwueke Kelechi who helped me with most of the illustrations

When the rain is falling, and the weather is cold, just make yourself a coffee and read some messages from flowers.

CONTENTS

For everyone breathing

HOLD ON,

Before you start

I want you to smile

and take a deep breathe

because you are about to feel alive

Today is not another day,

today is a day for you.

so stretch your body like a cat and

listen to the cracks of your bones,

yawn like you've starved for centuries,

fart like only you exist,

take shower and run to the bedroom

naked while nobody watches,

dress-up and wear those shoes,

then look at the mirror, smile and love yourself.

-live alive

It takes your breathe to make you stay alive,

but it takes the sky to make you feel alive.

So look up to the blue sky

and form shapes with the white clouds.

-stay alive

When you stare at the mirror,

listen to that voice that says "I'm great"

Don't create a stagnant life

out of these running days,

crawling months,

and moving years

else you are exhausting our oxygen

in vain.

If there is something more important than anything, it is you.

You are an Angel.

This is not a metaphor,

it's a theory.

heavens proved it.

After the moments now,

the next comes it a memory.

So choose how you want now

to be remembered.

Now is the future you have

been waiting for

Stay with people who will rise in the east like the sun when you face west, because they will shine light at your back for your shadow to get bigger in the front.

In a place far from home,

someone wishes to have an angel like you

whose wings will protect their hearts,

whose presence will absent all devils,

whose words will comfort their souls,

whose sword will shatter their sorrows

and dip them in the oceans of flame.

    -distant dreams;

    -a reminder that the world needs you

Life loves us so much

that he wakes us up

from a death called sleep

yet we are blind of this love.

Life gave us life,

gave us dreams,

and gave us energy.

So how is life not fair?

-wondering

we are burdened by the things we didn't say.

Expression makes us feel free,

and everybody is art.

They killed their dreams by sleeping

-For the ones who gave up on their dreams.

I lost sleep

but I'm still dreaming.

it feels so sweet to sleep when

the body gets tired, because the

mind usually goes with it

When you question your world,

always remember that the skies have the answer

and breathe is all you need.

-reminder

Exhale fear,

inhale faith.

Vomit diffidence,

swallow confidence.

Spit sorrows,

and sip bliss

Then you will never hungry anymore.

water the gardens

of your heart

with your tears

for they will

nutrify the flowers

and they may yield roses

Mi Aliento

I'm climbing a mountain

and I'm halfway to the peak

as my body sweats like a fountain

with pores too weak

but I won't ever stop climbing

because the vibrant fears of my soul

could not even enough

burn like a coal

because what it's made of

worth more treasures than gold

Your soul is a warrior

and your mind is a knight.

Fight with them not sword.

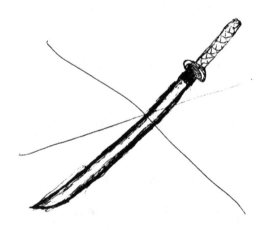

I'm a rose

that grew out of a thorn,

I trust my powers.

-believe in yourself

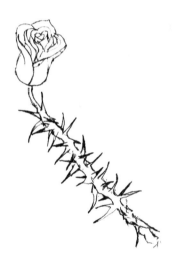

The way you love thinking small is the
way I love thinking big, because I have the
ambition of a little child wishing for big
houses with swimming pools in it

Ignorance devoured the eyes of our wit,

now he is crying bloods with no eyeballs

and having insomnia with empty eyes.

if ignorance was fortunes,

many would be rich

If we say we are bored,

how about the dead?

-wondering

Man was created to be immortal,

but the mortal taste of apple

made immortal man mortal.

I wish I had the taste of immortality,

I believe I might feel like a god.

-wishes

Bird of Jove,

strongest of its kind,

spread your wings

to both ends of the earth

and take me away.

   -feel like disappearing

The world gave you imagination

but you refused to fly

-for the ones blaming life

Sometimes I wish our body could travel

with our imagination,

to stay with us wherever imagination takes us.

   -wishes

Solitude is a place

where treasures are found

I'm not usual

because I promised change

as all I could offer

-feeling strange

I lack words

I admit that.

But I don't lack actions

because my body is alive.

-Feeling speechless.

I cannot be perfect

because perfection does not exist.

It only lives in our eyes.

I rained all energy

but it was still summer

-vain efforts

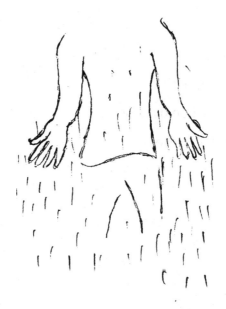

I can't see myself in the mirror

because the mirror is just a reflection of my body.

I can only see myself when my eyes are closed

and my ears pays attention to the

rhythm of my heartbeat.

I lust for those feelings

when it's flowing

and I'm writing.

-for all of us who use pen to fight

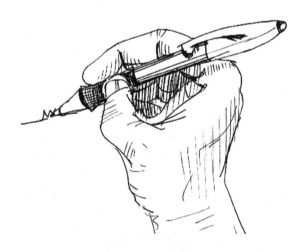

Those tears we didn't shed

bleeds in us.

Though they may dry with time

but their marks remain forever.

Those words you never said

lasted forever

The words you said to me

planted flowers in my head

and they grew trees on my mind.

The night is always noisy

when I'm not sleeping

because my silence talks a lot

Mind is a Fidus Achates

Creativity held me captive

In its Den of creation

and I couldn't get out of it.

Creativity is captivity

Dear Miss,

If beauty magazine makes you feel ugly,

write a beauty magazine

describe what beauty is

then you will realize you are beautiful.

For the ones feeling ugly

My hands, as white as snow,

my conscience, too crystal

for my soul to feel guilty

-Feeling innocent

Valley of crowned kings,

city of giants,

mountain of uncrowned queens,

clan of hobbits

are all your heart is made of.

    -Soft words

It's so encouraging to live

when what we could expect at the

end of this life is death

isn't it?

I will smile till I can smile no more

I will laugh till I can laugh no more

I will read till I can read no more

I will write till I can write no more

and I will live till I can live no more.

-for the ones living their lives

Move away with a dream,

permit no alibis for failure,

then come back with success.

If we set free what's inside,

we will fly.

because it's what's inside

that burdens our wings.

What's between us

is not distance,

it's energy

emitting through our souls.

I know you want an Angel who can watch over your soul while your body sleeps, I know you want someone who can carry your heart in their palms like it's an egg, I know you want someone who can kiss your lips while you are sleeping, I know you want someone who will kiss your lips when you wake up, I know you want someone who will always cuddle you from behind, I know you want someone who misses you, I know you want someone who can say sorry when they are wrong, I know you want someone whose text increases your heartbeat, I know you want someone who can understand the things you didn't say, I know you want someone who can make you up when you are asleep, I know you want someone who can listen to your stupid jokes and laugh even when you tell it twice, I know I can't write all you want, but all I know is that you want to be surrounded by love.

The loving times

I starred at you

like a piece of painting hanging on the wall.

But shyness made me look away

when cupid told you what I was doing

as your eyes glanced on me

   -crushing

"Will it cost you a dime if I slept under

the blanket of your love?"

She asked.

"Love is in the tiny air,

it's in the breeze,

you can feel it when it passes around,

not when you are under a blanket"

-*he said.*

You devoured my heart with your beauty,

eroded my imagination with your smile,

and burnt my heart with the flames of your love.

Now I'm left with ashes pumping you to my vein

-you have totally taken over me

You are just like the sky,

close when looking at

but far to reach.

   -*crushing*

Just like the moon,

you only passed at night to say *hello*.

every night, I waited for you,

starring through my window

to receive your *hello*.

But tonight was rainy,

and raindrops never allowed you to say *hello*.

Yet as you appear blur from afar,

I still received your *hello*,

and smiled goodnight.

    -the crushing

I wish I could allow my mouth

to speak my mind,

you would have understood my heart.

From the ones who only said 'I love you' with their souls.

A lip such as mine,

as arid as desert,

has not tasted the moist of yours.

Please save me the pains of biting my lips in the thirst of yours by reducing the margin between us, else my lips will be wounded by me.

-*crushing*

I was forced to crash your lips with mine

by the pressures of love,

put not the blame on me.

    -Irresistibility

When we met

our souls toasted glasses

to celebrate the discovery

of a perfect match

I don't believe in superstitions,

but I did when you appeared in the sky of my life

and the rain stopped falling.

You are my rainbow.

You never sailed before,

but I made you my captain.

Then we lost together

and never bothered

searching for our way back.

-just me and you-

My life was arid.

but when I met you,

I became a plant

transplanted from the desert

to the rainforest.

I bloomed and yielded flowers

because you watered me

You smiled,

and it lasted forever.

You hugged me,

and I felt atmospheres in my heart

with a cool breeze,

swirling in my stomach.

Sometimes I want to hold your hands,

look into your eyes,

say *I love you* with my heart,

and prove it with my lips

I counted the stars

and my palms itched me.

They were millions in the sky,

but I only saw a supernova.

You are the greatest thing

that's ever happened to me.

Brighter days are made of

morning suns,

blues skies,

coffees,

sunflowers,

and your kiss in my memories.

Good mornings are better said with your kisses

and a stare at your shape as you

prepare the breakfast

messages from flowers

love him like your life; for life is so dear

adore her like your best shoes;

for shoes protect the feet

respect him like your belief; for ones beliefs

are respected more than anything

keep her like a vow; for vows we don't break

cherish him like a value; for values are precious

listen to her like your thoughts; for one

never fails to listen to thoughts

hold his arms like a staff; for staffs are

gripped hard to support walking

kiss her lips like a lollipop; for lollipops are

sweet to the tongue and wets dry lip

remember him like your birthday; for

one never forgets their birthday

giver her flowers on a rainy day; for

it will make her feel warm

get jealous when his mom calls; for you will

want to be his mom in the shape of you

softly tell her 'I love you' on a sunny day;

for words like that comforts the soul

-an ode to the lovers

Sometimes I give thoughts to your words,

and smile.

It makes me come alive

-Moments of abstraction

The consolation of galaxies,

is all of you.

In a mysterious world

full of fantasies

where no nightmares exist,

we always met.

-dreams

If we could look at the bright

side of everything,

we will be unfamiliar with happiness

North and south poles attract,

but that's not same with our hearts.

It's only same with our lips.

Your voice became so fond of me

such that I still hear us talking

even when the conversation has ended.

Just like the harmonies of nature's sounds in silence,

your voice pampered me to slumber

-the stories you told

Nothing was better than those moments

when we stayed together

and our silence did the talking.

-reminiscing

I saw the shape of you in the dark shades of

the moon last night and became jealous

because I want to be the only one

who knows the shape of you.

-jealous love

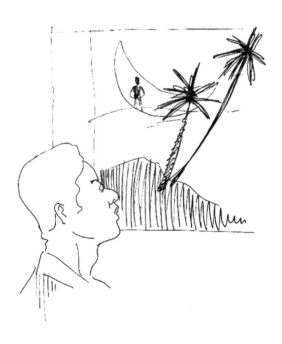

God sent you to me because he knows I'm

always envious when I read stories about

people who saw angels in the bible.

Conscience never lied,

only words did

Your smiles

makes me wonder

why you are not

among the stars

in the galaxies

I will still live in you

even when you are gone

because you are my world.

Sometimes I look at your pictures

and whisper *I love you* to your ears

hoping you can hear me wherever you are

   -*missing you*

You said to me 'I love you' only at nights.

But I want to hear those words in the morning

when the sun wakes us up

as she shines through the window

radiating on our skin.

   -soft words

The seven colors of the rainbow

were mixtures of you

because that was all my eyes could see.

-blinded by you

You were a song,

but I'm not a singer.

You said 'sing',

but my voice only knew your name.

Maybe what you want is a tone

but all I have is a pen.

I'm just a writer.

The world is made up of 7 billion people,

but you came

and made it 8 billion.

Will it weird if I undress and dance in the rain?

-She asked

Forgive me for calling you a princess

for I never knew you are royalty itself

sometimes when I look at you

I feel like you are a picture

stolen from the gallery of art

sometimes when I look at you

I feel like you are hidden wisdom

stolen from an ancient scroll

sometimes when I look at you

I feel like you are a gemstone

stolen from Sierra Leone

-what I see when I look at you

To that one person who you can run to,

hug and dry your tears in their shirts

Maybe the life we want to live

does not exist.

But if you believe in us,

we can create it.

-soft words

"How did you find me?", She asked.

"Your heart is my compass,

your destination is my bearing,

I will never get lost searching for you".

He said.

You only smiled to make me feel good,

but those smiles never came from your heart.

I want smiles that you don't have.

True smiles

that comes from the heart.

Sing to me a lullaby

so that I may fall asleep in your arms

to dream about you.

But when I wake up,

will you still be there singing?

or will I see you gone?

Dear Mr. Lover

Our lips had an accident

and your lips tasted like

the vitamins from the words of Shakespeare

-romantic confessions

You walked your fingers on my back

and I felt Angels

-romantic confessions

I have never felt anything

as soft as what's found beneath your neck.

-Romantic confessions

The Hercules between your legs

was like Thor's hammer

pounding my cervix

till milks produced

   -the love we made in her head

I felt the heat

as our hips made sounds,

because energy flow was constant

before climax arrived.

  -hybrid love we made

"Let's share your loneliness

maybe we can create out of it

happiness that will last forever"

She said.

When you smiled,

I saw many tears hidden in it

because everything you didn't say

was louder to my ear

-for connected souls

"Hit any part of my body with your lips,

I want to feel some pains of your romantic pleasure"

she said

Love is a battle between two souls

who want to break the void of being strangers

but the heart is not an honest soldier

I am sick at heart

because my heart pumps love

instead of blood

Twilight

My favorite colors of the sky are not in the rainbows, they are colors from the light of the sky at the end of the day when the night is still young, and the day gone old. Because after that your love takes over and rule the night.

I used to call you better

when I haven't found the word *'perfect'*

Perfection is a feeling we get in

the palms of the right ones

The moon completed her phases

and the stars hid behind the dark clouds.

Now the songs of the insects rule the night

and I'm lonely on my bed trying to picture your face

but I couldn't,

because your face was in the stars

-missing you

The bed feels cold without you,

summers are rainy without you,

parties are lonely without you,

and I'm full like space without you.

-loneliness

I wish you could see the truth in my lies,

the songs in my heart,

the words in my silence,

the energy in my heartbeat,

the bravery in my fears,

and the joys in my tears.

You would know they are all for you

and all by you.

    -wishes

Your eyes are reflective and transparent,

I can see myself in it

and I can see your heart through it.

You can't hide anything from me.

-for connected souls

I received your messages before you sent it

because the stars were watching you

and I was watching the stars.

·for connected souls

You wrapped my hands around your neck,

took me to my favorite destination

just to kiss me and say goodbye.

but when I woke up,

I saw you sleeping beside me.

Oh, what a Nightmare!

-The nightmare

Time was never more precious than you

because art made you with shinning stones

and beauty designed you with jewels.

-too beautiful

I just want to let you know that;

your grins have occupied my memories,

your shape has filled my imagination,

and your beauty is an amaranth.

-reminder

Confidence is a gift from maturity

"You took me to a missionary journey

in the land of pleasures

where I felt your energy"

She said.

-our love memories running in her head

I'm having a great trip

exploring the vast continent

of your love

with wild waters

and blue seas

the tired walls of my palms

finds it's comfort lying on your chest

the deaf drums of my ear

finds it's comfort listening to your voice

the fragile hairs of my head

finds it's comfort resting on your laps

the sad looks of my face

finds it's comfort gazing at your smile

the depressed stares of my eyeballs

finds it's comfort looking at your face

the arid lips of my mouth

finds it's comfort resting on yours

the weak veins of my body

finds it's comfort embracing your hugs

the fearful breathes of my nose

find it's comfort leaning on your shoulders

it is in you, that my comfort lies

   -where my comfort lies

Your heart is the paradise I've been looking for

thanks for letting me find it.

-grateful for your love

You are my clock

when you smile, I will know it's morning

when you laugh, I will know it's afternoon

and when you cry, I will know it's night.

Thanks for telling me the time.

What distracts me

is how you pay attention

-romantic confession

I was still dreaming of you

when you crawled on my lips like an eel

and kissed good morning.

  -best way to wake me up

I hate when goodbyes are not said with

kisses to depart us to home after work.

-love at workplace

Venus presided over you

then art ruined you

-you are too beautiful

"On this rock I will build my house"

She said to me leaning on my chest

pointing at my heart

House of lords,

Empire of emperors,

Palace of kings and queens,

are all in your heart.

And that is where my home is.

Love is not blind,

Love sees all scars

Love sees all injuries

Love sees all faults

Love sees all weaknesses

but accepts all.

Take love with you

anywhere you go.

It will protect you

and shed you from the dangers of hate.

Love weakens hatred,

then love conquers.

The breaking
and
The hurting times

Just like a supernova,

their hearts exploded,

and their love sparkled.

Then suddenly,

all faded away.

We fell in love on a rainy day

but summer broke us up

because you only loved me when it's cold outside

so that I can keep you warm inside.

It started like it will never end,

we departed from being two stranger souls

to becoming one familiar soul.

But now,

what's found when love is lost

is keeping us apart.

Looking at myself

all I see is you.

"how can I not see myself anymore?

when did I become you?"

    I asked to no answer.

If you cannot see what's inside,

don't fall in love with what's outside.

They blow off their candles as they leave

so that you will not see with the lights from it

anymore

You left

and the leaves waved goodbye.

I didn't want to do the same,

but my eyes were stubborn

because my heart couldn't endure.

I cry because it lessens my sorrows.

But it never brought joy to me.

She said

You left,

and my heart was nowhere to be found

because you took it with you

You said I'm your angel,

but angels are white and I'm looking blue

because your tongue is an artist

that paints with blue color.

-sadness

You promised me to the moon and back,

But when you got to the moon

I became earth in yours eyes.

You only passed by the night to say *hi*

and you were never back.

You promised not to break my heart

but you made it bleed.

As my blood is dripping

hope you find pleasures in it?

A fragile heart

shattered by a broken promise.

A salty tongue

produce no sour words

but that as sweet as honey

to convince the ears

you created a photo album in my head

which gives me memories of blinking tears

whenever I view them

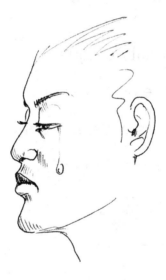

You were never taught how to love

then breaking hearts became part of you

I hate sleeping on my bed because it's full of memories that makes me remember how your fingers drove circularly on my jewel. And I can't endure my eyes to rain when this movie starts playing in my head, especially when it gets to the ending scenes.

You live in some part of me

even though I didn't create room for you

-confessions

You concluded the breakup message

with *have a nice day*.

what was on your mind when you said that?

I told you that my heart

was made of glasses,

yet you threw stones.

This shirt makes me feel nostalgic whenever I wear it

because it has memories of you

-things you left in me

I stopped listening to the music

when it started talking about you

because I didn't want to see

my broken pieces anymore.

Yet I couldn't decline the picture

because there is no delete button

to wipe it off my memory

Maybe cupid shot us

but you broke the arrow that bond us.

Love was as tiny as air

before you made it vulnerable

then it started hurting

like the heat of Sulphur

Seasons change,

right ones turn to wrong ones,

then our hearts break.

My heart is always open.

I never shut or locked it,

because 'knocking' hurts my soul.

Then it became a passage for strangers

travelling to unknown lands to find love.

who come in from the front door

and move out through the back door

making sure they pick a piece of me before leaving.

My heart was an empire

where you ruled as an emperor,

but made me a slave.

In every single tear I drop

lies a misery caused by you.

hope you find paradises in them.

The effect of your words,

were goosebumps on my body.

I was like a child,

I couldn't realize

they were utterings of deceit

till pendant turned to dagger

and jabbed my heart.

I emitted three words with my tongue.

"That is not what I want", He said.

and my heart got injured

I had the thing he doesn't want.

I had love.

Your heart, as light as mercury

but pure like a mud.

I hate goodbyes

because they still come by

to live in our memories

I travelled three thousand light years

through the milky way

to get to your heart,

but only an explode

got me back to earth.

Your heart was never a place for me.

I was an alien in your heart.

I've been crying all night

not because you left me,

but because you left without saying goodbye.

I wished to hear your voice for the last time,

because it was the melody for my soul.

Just like a rose flower rejected on a valentine's day,

you made me look worthless.

I am sorry for making those beautiful skies
in your eyes rain. Please dip my deeds in the
oceans of your raindrops so that my blemishes
may bathe away, and flow to the dry lands
where it will be absorbed by the thirsty sands
-my sincere words

   -remorse

I broke your heart;

my lips trembled,

my ribs cracked,

and your tears caused earthquakes

in my heart

-confessions

-remorse

A thousand words from your silence

explains how heavy your eyes are

and how light your heart is.

As those tears roll down from your eyes,

let them wash away my wrongs from your sight

and erode the aches I caused, from your heart.

-My sincere words.

-remorse

Love is a credit to the soul

but heartbreak is a debit to the heart

because debit robs credit.

Hugs are free,

smiles are free,

kisses are free,

but love is costly.

The healing times

When Autumn comes,

the leaves fall off.

That's how time heals the wounds.

I am here

because I was lost

searching for a guardian Angel

and that's what I've become.

I was a fallen Angel with broken wings, my legs had no strength to carry me, my eyes stopped bleeding tears because my mouth became too weak to cry. But with the little strength in my arms, I picked up my broken pieces and bond them together. Then I became a lonely Angel with growing wings, and that was when I found myself.

Love is a wound

Love is a healer

Love is a weapon

Love is a fighter

but now he's on exile

My heart was a good audient,

all he wanted was the dramas of love

acted on the stage of affection.

But you played the role of a villain

and offered him the show of violence.

Then he disappeared,

For he adored not your offer.

You angered my heart

and the sun set in the east.

You thought I was just a comet,

unaware I'm all the galaxies

I was the host

to your parasite,

but now

you are struggling to live

in the tiny air

I stopped molding my heart

when I realized it gets broken into pieces

at the end.

What confuses me is how we let our

hearts fall in love with a body

Instead of a soul

If I had used the mirrors,

I wouldn't have loved myself anymore

after you shattered me into fragments

because all I could have seen was you.

Your smiles are so costly

yet you give them out freely

to the ones who don't need it

Don't tell me you have oceans of love

because I can't swim the ocean

It could have stopped me

because it took every part of my imagination.

but it dissolved into the tiny air

when I realized it was just a mirage

-breakup thoughts

You sank my heart

and my feelings went with it.

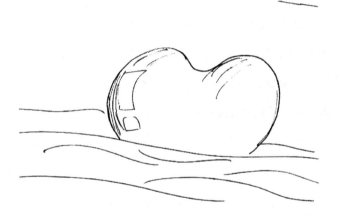

my heart was a white blank page

who needed some delicious words

to occupy it's emptiness

but you shaded it with dark ink

and tore it into two.

I was lonely

when I was with you.

My life was vacuum with you,

but when you were gone,

my life was filled without you.

"Give me a piece of you, for I can't

feel complete without it"

-he said.

"If I gave every piece of me to every you I met,

the only thing that would have remained of me

would be my bones and my nothing".

-she said.

Seeing you reminds me of my dad

that's why I don't want to loosen my heart

because it might be treated like my mom's

-she said

Dear Mister,

I am never your everything,

I am just your one thing

among your everything.

Do remember that.

-yours truly,

-lover

Love never says goodbye.

Even when you are healed from his

heartbreak, he still leaves pieces of his

photos stamped in your memories

so that he can bring them to your sight

during reminiscing moments

After breakup,

we make rules not to fall in love anymore,

but the eyes and the heart make this rule useless

because they still get drunk and succumb to love.

I believe in the death and resurrection of emotions

-*loving again*

The voices

They had no voice to speak

so they gave me pen to write their minds

-the speechless

My mum possesses a disease called worry.

this disease is pandemic to all mums

because they are born with it

and it's incurable.

Sometimes dads contract this disease from mums

but often drink it away.

   -mums worry a lot

I want to give you a knife

so that you can rip-off that thought

telling you not to love yourself.

I want to give you button

so that you can mute that voice in your

head, telling you, you are not beautiful.

I want to give you a scarf

so that you can blindfold those eyes in

you, that sees inferiority in you.

Will you accept my offer?

-from the positives in us

My tongue is sweating of words,

but no one to speak to.

-from the wise man

Your words are treasures to my soul

but mysteries to my ear.

Verbalize to me, more of your diamonds

for my soul cherishes your treasures.

-to that one person I always listen to

Your words are my carbohydrates,

speak more to me

for my soul needs more energies

-*Message from my soul to that one who encourages me*

In the secrecy of my own heart,

I will live, till I go to the empire of spirits at the other

side of the sun where no traveler returns, with the

words you told me that you want no ear to attend,

hoarded and slaved in the prison of my heart.

-a promise with no yoke

If you've ever told your secret to me,

This is for you.

In a world such as ours,

mysterious, ridiculed and puzzled,

only the sphinx and the Hercules survive.

The king is dead,

long live the king.

That's how the society is;

full of ironies and delusions.

A question of why

demands an answer of reason

not alibis

If I have ever lied to you,

sorry it was my creativity.

She never wants me to get cut

because straight trees

are cut before the narrow ones.

If I'm hot, do not pour water on me

for it will bring out more heat from me,

and you might not withstand the intensity.

So allow the cool breeze to calm me down,

for It will be better than water.

-from the hot tempered

I wish 4 a.ms lasts forever

-*wishes from the morning larks*

My sickness could be cured,

if only you lay your hands on the strings.

For music is for the soul,

and thy rhythm heals my soul.

-from the music lovers

My lips are starving of yours,

my balloons are missing your mild fingers,

my shoulder is suffering from hotness

due to lack of your cool breathe.

my scabbard is hollowly open and agitated,

come and fill it with your sword

and calm it with your frozen milk.

Because all will not be still

unless they eat their foods.

-From the aroused lady to his lover

Their voices came from the dry leaves

lying aridly in the woods,

a choir of sad tones lifelessly singing:

our souls were pure,

our minds were free,

and our hands were innocent,

for us to deserve this.

so why depart us from a world

that we were meant to be?

-*From the bitter voices of aborted children*

Everyone has an inner audient

that listens to them

when the inner orator speaks.

So, speak to me with your heart

For I will be there listening.

For I am thy inner audient.

-From subconscious mind

You listened but didn't hear,

looked but never saw.

only if you were a me,

you could have been a you.

I am infinite, my name is intelligence.

I am the river that the birds kiss when they are thirsty.

And I love it when they deep themselves

in me and shake their heads and flap

their wings to refreshen their bodies

because it makes me see the love I can offer.

I want to be the lake in the desert,

so that travelers will drink from me

and satisfy the thirst of their donkeys with my energy.

In a land where no valleys exist,

I am the fire that burns on the mountain.

In a garden where no flowers exist,

I am the rose that sprouts from a thorn.

In a rainforest where no holocaust occurs,

I am the flame that dries the wet leaves.

I am the rain in the summer days

and the ice in the desert.

I melt my body to give water to the thirsty sand.

I am weightless,

as light as feather

such that an empty bag

can stand upright than me.

-Feeling totally empty and exhausted

I am trapped in the roman colosseum,

I need a gladiator to fight for me

for my life is not only in danger

but also on the fence between thorns and den

Oh heavenly Angels!

I hope you heard my cry?

-in need of miracles

between Scylla and Charybdis

is where I am now.

Let my soul look for the wise man

to make a choice.

I am stuck in the island of curiosity,

only imagination can get me out.

Only mortals are afraid to die

our souls are not the same.

Infidelity is a king

that can crown an April's gentleman a knight

by kneeling him before humiliation and abasement

Wounds that don't bleed,

hurts the most.

Eyes that don't cry,

cries the most.

Mouths that don't speak,

talks the most.

They all do it within.

"Depart from what you cannot be part" Says the rain.

listen to it as it patters on your roof,

for it will not last forever.

There is nothing more

found in an idle brain

than ignorance

Inquisitiveness distracted me,

shrouded me in the optimism of curiosity,

and led me to the kingdom of enthusiasm.

Now I can't find my way back home.

Forgive me o Lord!

for I have committed adultery

by lusting for knowledge.

We your offspring have broken your jurisprudences,

burnt down your advice and threw them into Nile,

heeded to no proverbs of yours

and sang no canticles of your choir.

Please do not loose hold your wrath,

nor unfasten your tongue,

nor set sail thy sword.

For if thy do so,

hades will be friendlier than what will befall us.

Oh high council of heavens!

pardon us our trespasses.

-Sympathy for the world and empathy for the heavens

I was weak of my own strengths,

a fool of my own wisdom,

a coward of my own hero,

a sabotage of my own Bournes,

and a whistle-blower of my own secrets.

I built myself a house on harum-scarum

and slaved myself in the freedoms of alibis.

But now, I have laid judgements on myself,

by being the prosecutor and the jury

just to realize to my own surprise,

that I am my own enemy.

If I would be merciful, I will owe myself a forgiveness.

-Remorse on myself for my mistakes.

Oh four ancient elements,

flame my sorrows to ashes,

wet my dry bones,

sip my tears,

and evolve my agonies to heavens.

For I am debilitated by the pandemoniums of life.

-Feeling weak and painful

when struck by the tragedies of life.

Lamp of heaven,

the smiling star at night,

and the mother of the galaxies.

Light my inner soul

so that I may glitter like you

to give my light to the world.

-talking to the moon

My shadow has always been my best friend,

he stays behind and fixes me when I'm broken,

he always said things that made me smile,

he always speaks in my silence,

sometimes he pranks me by getting bigger,

sometimes when I don't see him,

I thought he had left me.

But he never did, he only became invisible

and he is always there.

-I love my shadow

Fear feasts on the famine of faith,

hatred feasts on the famine of admiration,

distrust feeds on the famine of trust,

and lust feeds on the famine of love.

Our greatest fear

is the one we create

and make the greatest

I used to think that people who fall

in love does it intentionally,

I used to say that lovers are dumb,

I used to believe that people who cry are weak,

I used to mock people who do stupid

things in the name of love,

I used to believe that people who say

I miss you are too emotional,

I used to do all these and more,

but now, I don't do them anymore

because I have seen the world as they did.

-forgive my thoughts

Do not feel inferior when I understand

your puzzles so quickly

than you ever thought

because maybe we think alike

while others think together

-from all of us who think strange to all of us who think strange

They will take your loyalty as weakness,

take your sincerity as foolishness,

take your obedience as cowardliness.

But I assure you;

amongst them, you are the bravest.

-Messages from flowers

Sometimes we come organized,

sometimes we come scattered

so that you can pick us

and assemble us

·from inspirations

Spirit of ancestors

speak to my ear

for I am sitting on these noisy leaves

beneath your foot

ready to listen

and hear what your mouth has for us.

-meditating

I picked up an ember from a heap of ashes

in the brightest hour of the day,

ceaselessly blew air to it,

to keep it alive and make it shine at nights

when it's glowing light will be

visible even to the blind,

but all it could do was to burn my palms.

'should I have poured water on it?',

I asked to no answer.

-Regrets of getting bad returns for good deeds

Maybe they hate the fairer sex because they
are full of delusional thoughts that the fairer
sex is weak. Yet even with their thoughts,
they still hate their fellow sterner sex.

Maybe they hate the fairer sex because they are
cynical about them. Yet even with their believes,
they are still cynical about their fellow sterner sex.

They have built themselves houses laid
on the foundation of illusions

And have conditioned their senses to translate
facts into misconceptions because that's the
only thing their brains can accommodate.

I just want to let them know that the
fairer sex brought them to life.

And they were like eggs in the hands of the fairer
sex before they hatched and become young dragons
that grew to monsters and hate what gave them life.

   -to the misogynists

You told me to follow your footsteps,

but you walked on the snows

and when the sun came out

I got lost.

you told me to follow your footsteps

but you walked on the desert sands

and when the storm came

I got lost.

How do you consider yourself a paragon

while your steps lead people to lost?

-to the ones who mislead us

Even liars love to hear the truth

When I needed water,

the skies cried.

When I needed music,

the birds sang.

When I needed honey,

the bees urinated.

When I needed warmth,

the sun raised his head and smiled.

When I needed light in the dark,

the moon and the stars went naked.

When I needed milk,

the cows lactated.

When I needed shelter,

the trees bent.

With all these,

how can I hate nature,

than to love her more?

when my thirst was sour and dry,

the rain came down nobly

showering for the rescue of my throat

when my eyes were filled with

vacancy and scantiness,

the rainbow appeared ghostly in the sky

glowing to the rescue of my sight

when my soul was soaked with frustrations and panic,

sleep cuddled me like a blanket

and dimmed me to rest

for the rescue of my eyelids

when my nose was filled with the storms of desert,

the cool breeze exhaled gently

blowing for the rescue of my breathe.

with all these I ask;

how can I hate nature, than to love her more?

The sky frowned,

her face went dark,

and I was pampered to sleep as she cried.

But woke up when I stopped

hearing melodies in my dreams

just to realize she is not crying anymore.

-rainfall

whenever the sky is crying,

I always see little children bathing away their

sorrows with the tears of the sky as they

dance to the rhythm of their happiness.

They rejoice when thunder adds bass to the rhythm

and shouts for joy when lightning

turns on the party lights.

   -children dancing in the rain is happiness

The skies feel happy when the rainbow is out because it dries their tears.

Why do we burden our heads

with loads that can break our neck

when feathers are there to carry?

A watchman who narrates the

dreams he had during the night

fires himself from his job

Most of our sufferings are self-inflicted

Dear heroes behind the shadows,

your death gave us life,

your violence gave us tranquility,

your bloods watered our lands,

you bought war to sell peace,

you starved so that we can eat,

you left and never returned so that we may stay

and you absorbed bullets for the

exchange of our pleasures.

If the living could relate with the dead, we

would have offered more than diamonds.

But all we could offer were roses on your gravestones,

and tears on our bitter faces.

Your names are written in our hearts and

your pictures stamped on our memories.

We promise that one day, when we shall meet at

the other side of the sun where no journey reverts,

we shall bring to you, a chicken for your

table and a wine for your dinner.

But until that day,

your glory remains immortal, in our

hearts, and on earth where you lived.

Dedicated to all soldiers who fought for freedom and peace

You traded sorrow for happiness,

traded indigence for riches,

and traded tears for smiles.

You possessed a virus called kindness

which fed your appetite with gratification.

Selflessness was all you craved for,

but respect and admiration followed you

everywhere, cheering you as you triumphed.

Deep in our hearts, shall your names live long,

not as that on the sand dunes, but

like that written on a stone.

-For the ones called patrons

Armageddon

This is where it's all going to end.

In an amphitheatre bigger than roman colosseum,

people cheering, yelling sounds rising, voices roaring,

kings and queens of light and darkness seated,

our bodies moving around on earth,

while our souls absent from it

seated as spectators watching the last combat

as happiness fights sadness,

joy fights sorrow,

bliss fights grief,

affluent fights indigence

soothe fights worry,

and heaven fights misery

with their elite soldiers armed with two

edged sword as sharp as thistle

jabbing and eliminating the soldiers of dark forces.

The end of this battle shall determine

the permanent state of mankind,

but it is certain that good shall never be won by evil.

Then at the end, good shall rule over all.

From out of this war, bliss shall emerge as a virus,

and all mankind shall possess it and live with it.

And then, we will be free again.

Dear friend,

your name has finally found it's home in my pen,

and my mouth derives peace in calling your name;

Theophilus. I know, I know nothing, because I have

committed adultery by lusting for knowledge. I pray

heavens borrow me a forgiveness so that I may pay

the debt of my sins, even though I might sin again.

But at this moment, Theophilus, I assure you that our

feet are happy for finally arriving successfully to the

destination of a journey taken from hope. march-

off the dusts off your feet, wash your feet with the

oceans of your tears and allow the sky to dry them.

Now from here, we will not depart but shall meet

again when smiles have eroded sadness from

our faces and happiness slaved in our hearts.

   -from me to you with kind regards

I write for all of us who don't have words,

and for all of us who have words

but has no mouth to speak

-*Igaegburumnwa Emmanuel*

ABOUT THE AUTHOR

Igaegburumnwa Emmanuel is a poet and a storyteller. He fell in love with Music, history and literature at the age of sixteen. He is popularly known by his funny surname 'Igaegburumnwa' which was later (but not publicly) shortened to 'Igaems' as a result of the difficulty people had in pronouncing it. You can find him on Instagram @igaegburumnwa_emmanuel.jr, Facebook @Igaegburumnwa Emmanuel Jr, Twitter @igaegburumnwa Emmanuel.jr, and Tumblr @Igaegburumnwa Emmanuel.

Printed in the United States
By Bookmasters